The Power of Perception

6 Steps to Behavior Change

Hyrum W. Smith

The Power of Perception

Copyright © 2013 by Hyrum Smith

ISBN (978-1-940498-00-3)

Printed in USA by Alexander's

Dedication

I am quite sure that each of us has someone, or a few people, in our lives that have made a significant contribution to making us who we are today. These are often teachers, coaches, parents, siblings, childhood friends, colleagues at work, religious leaders, or just plain folks that have been there at a crucial time in our lives and pointed us in the right direction.

One of those great human beings for me is man named Jerry Pulsipher. Our paths first crossed in 1962 and 1963 in London England. Since that time we have worked together on many projects. He has helped me wright several books. He was one of the team that discovered the reality model and helped me to discover its power.

This book is dedicated to him. Shakespeare said it best: "Tis human fortunes happiest height to be a spirit melodious, lucid, poised and whole. Second in order of felicity is walk with such a soul.

Jerry is a great and noble soul, without whom this book would not exist. Thank you Jerry for leading the way for me.

Table of Contents

Foreword

I have had the incredible privilege of working with two of the most brilliant thought leaders of our time: Stephen R. Covey and Hyrum Smith. I have worked closely with both men and their influence has molded my career and enhanced my personal life.

I met Hyrum when Covey Leadership Center and Franklin Quest merged. I came from the "other side," the Covey Leadership Center side. I had heard a lot of urban legends about the great Hyrum Smith and how he was bigger than life, a renaissance man, a master of persuasion, a consummate entertainer, and I discovered he is all that.

As I came to know Hyrum through working with him on his books and other projects I saw another side: a kinder and gentler side, a thoughtful and introspective side, and a real person with real troubles and real challenges. I have seen Hyrum walk the talk; I have watched him apply the Power of Perception to make positive personal and professional change in his own life. I have witnessed the Reality Model process bring him inner peace and success.

Understanding and using Hyrum's Reality Model provides me with the tool to examine my motives so that I too can make quantum leap changes in my life by making small adjustments.

I learned about Maslow's Hierarchy of Needs in high school psychology class and understand that we must satisfy each need in order starting at the bottom: biological and physiological. Only when the lower needs are met can we become concerned with the higher order of needs: influence and personal development. Stephen Covey suggests a similar model of effectiveness with the Maturity Continuum. Hyrum teaches his own hierarchy that mirrors Covey and Maslow but Hyrum takes us one level deeper: he introduces us to the concept that humans require variety

When I'm stuck in a rut and I'm doing the same thing day after day with no variety, I stagnate. I stop progressing. I become mired down in the thick of thin things. I spend more time in the quagmire of self-doubt, self-deception, and depression. I wholeheartedly agree with Hyrum that we require variety. I must examine the Reality Model and examine my perceptions, and my paradigms. The definition of insanity is doing the same thing over and over and expecting different results. When we see the world through a different lens, then we behave differently and ultimately achieve different results.

I can only assume that you are reading this book because you're in the same place. You want variety from the routine, the mundane, and the rut of spinning your wheels and so you're considering making some behavior and life changes. So I sincerely invite you to open your heart to Hyrum's Power of Perception. I guarantee that if you apply these principles, you will see an increase in work productivity, you'll experience more fulfilling and rewarding relationships, and here you'll find a deeply personal inner peace.

As I came to know Hyrum's background and to know his lovely wife Gail I realized how truly blessed I am to have learned the power of changing my life by analyzing my perceptions through the Reality Model

Annie Howell-Oswald
Global Media Publishing Director

Preface

Back in the late 1980's the Franklin Quest company was growing at a meteoric pace. Franklin Planners began to appear all over the world. The impact that the planner and the time management seminar that went with it was creating remarkable change in those we taught.

Over ninety per cent of the people who began using the Franklin Planner would purchase the refill every year.

We became obsessed with the answer to the question:

"Why do they do that?" and then came the real question: "What causes permanent behavioral change?" As we continued to ask ourselves that question we discovered the reality model.

We didn't call it the Reality Model at first. It was just a visual way of describing what was going on in people's lives anyway. Jerry Pulsipher, to whom this book is dedicated, led the way in this discovery. None of us ever talked about creating the model, or inventing the model. It was always, "We discovered the Model."

I was so taken by the potential for good that the model had that I began giving what I call my Power of Perception speech all over the world. I was asked to present this speech at the SII (Securities Industry Institute) annual school held at the Wharton Business school in Philadelphia in the late eighties. I have been invited back to make the same speech to each new class for 24 years. The reception of the speech has been so positive we decided to turn it into a book.

So here it is. If you want to know why you do what you do and how to make changes that last forever this book is for you. When you have finished reading the Power of Perception you will likely want to invest in a large bottle of Windex.

Introduction
The Reality Model Promise

First, I want you to know that I take your commitment to read this book very seriously. I know the impact that adhering to the principles in this book can make in your life. And so I'm going ask you to do three things as you read.

1. Take notes. Write down or highlight everything that resonates with you.

2. When you have finished the book, take the next 36 hours and review, ponder and consider the notes you've taken. Just think about them.

3. Within 48 hours of finishing this book, teach what you have learned to one other person. This can be a spouse, friend, neighbor, associate, teenager, or someone on the bus.

If you'll do these three things, I will **guarantee** that you will see a marked and measurable change in how you make personal and professional decisions. Now that's a big promise to make before you've read anything, but I've had the opportunity of sharing this with a lot of people around the world. I'm very confident about what this book can do, if you'll do those three things. Do we have a deal? Read on.

Chapter One
Behavior Change

Basic Principles of Productivity

Think about the following statement:

The basic principles that help a human being become more productive and effective have not changed for 6,000 years.

Twenty-eight years ago, I, with my partners, started the Franklin Planner business. In that time, I have had the opportunity to teach a lot of time management seminars all over the world. Over the years, it has become common for numerous people to approach me before or after a presentation. They come up to me, lower their voices, look around to make sure nobody's listening then they say, "You know, Hyrum, I wish I lived a hundred years ago when they had more time."

"Really?" I responded, "How much more time did they have a hundred years ago?"

"Oh, they had a lot more time."

That is a common misperception. Do you know what the only difference is between today and a hundred years ago? The only difference is that today we have more options. Why do we have more options? Because we do things faster. As a technologically advanced culture, we are into speed.

If my grandfather missed a train, it was no big deal. He'd wait twenty-four hours and catch another train. If my father missed an airplane, no big deal he'd wait five hours and catch another airplane. If I miss one section of a revolving door, I go nuts. And so do you. Why do we do that? Because we want speed, that's why. Would you tolerate the speed of a computer fifteen years ago today?

The basic principles that help a human being become more productive and effective have not changed for 6,000 years.

Say it out loud. Write it down.

Every generation has to rediscover these principles. We give new names to them; we write books about them. A good friend of mine wrote a book, *The 7 Habits of Highly Effective People*. I wrote a book, *What Matters Most*. Read either book. There's not a new idea in either book. Why do I tell you this? What I'm going to be sharing with you in this book is really old stuff, it just happens to be very relevant for today. The magic of the 7 Habits is the fact that he put seven of them together. The magic is how they are taught for the 21st century. The basic principles go back a long way.

Now why do I make an issue of this? What hasn't changed in the last hundred or a thousand years? You and I. As human beings, we haven't changed. We still have to

14

go to the bathroom several times a day. We put our pants on one leg at a time. The human being is the same. What has changed? Our environment has changed. And it's changing at warp speed. The tools with which we implement these principles are changing fast. But the basic principles that help you and me become better, greater people haven't changed for a long time.

The process of how to learn these principles must be rediscovered in every generation by individuals and organizations. We explored this at Franklin Quest, the time management company I founded back in the 1980's.

Understanding Permanent Behavior Change

At Franklin Quest we became obsessed with this question: What causes permanent behavioral change? Carrying a planner around was a behavioral change. Why did six million people in 170 countries do that?

As we asked ourselves this question, a model surfaced that we all could agree upon. We decided to call that model the Reality Model. I got pretty excited about it and started giving reality model speeches all over the world.

I'm going to introduce you to the Reality Model today and make you dangerous with it. This model can, if you allow it to, change your life and the lives of all those with whom you share it. The foundation of the model is understanding the definitions of the 'real world' – principles, natural laws, and addictions.

The Real World Defined

The world as it really is might not be as we wish it were or think it should be. After I left Franklin Covey some friends and I started a new venture called The Galileo Initiative.

Why did we call our new little venture Galileo? Who was Galileo? He was an Italian physicist, mathematician, astronomer, and philosopher who played a major role in the Scientific Revolution. His achievements include improvements to the telescope and the consequent astronomical observations. Galileo has been called the "father of science."

Up until Galileo, most people in the western world believed that the earth was the center of the universe, and the sun went around the earth. Actually, in the early 16th century, it was Copernicus who first stated that the earth was revolving around the sun. He died in 1543, just twenty years before Galileo was born. With the exception of a few, no one took his theory seriously. Then here Galileo comes along and says, "Hey, I've improved the telescope! I've done the math! I can prove that the earth is going around the sun!"

How did the world react to this new concept? Galileo was beaten, flogged and excommunicated from his church. He spent the last 15 years of his life under house arrest as a condemned heretic. But he was right. He had the correct perception of the real world. That's what the Reality Model helps us do: it helps us to see the world it really is.

Before we get in to the nuts and bolts of the Reality Model, I would like to define three more words as they will be used in the Model.

Principles

Once we see how things really are, we begin to perceive the principles our beliefs are based upon. **Principles are what we believe to be true about ourselves, and what we believe about the world and our place in it.** The principles we follow don't change based on how our outside circumstance influence us. Correct principles can give us direction as we make life decisions. They are guideposts that help us successfully navigate the bombardment of change we are experiencing every day.

Natural Laws

Natural laws are fundamental patterns of nature and life that human experience has shown to be valid. Natural laws are rarely if ever changed or influenced to move in a different direction. We cannot change these laws to be what we want because they are universal and affect everyone. Choosing to accept these laws or not will have an impact on the choices we make and the consequences of those choices

Addiction

Here is my definition of addiction: **Addiction is compulsive behavior with short-term benefits and long-term destruction.** This is not a book on addiction. This is not a dictionary definition of addiction. The purpose of this definition will be very evident as you continue.

When I say the word addiction most people start thinking about drugs and alcohol. Those are in fact addictive behaviors. But alcoholism and drug abuse are only two of many different kinds of addictive behaviors. Think of other kinds of addictive behaviors. What are they? Exercise, work, eating! There are lots of different kinds of addictive behaviors.

Now that we have defined the real world, principles, natural laws, and addictions you are ready to be introduced to the Reality Model. As you read, remember these definitions. They will be instrumental in understanding and applying the model effectively.

Chapter Two
The Reality Model

Human Needs:

For now, mentally shelve these definitions. Go back and review them if you have to. Here is the Reality Model. There are five pieces to that model.

Look at the circle below: Human Needs. Now understand this fact: You have four powerful, driving human needs. Whether you think you've got them or not, you've got them. Psychologists have done all kinds of studies. They all say we have these four powerful human needs:

Human Needs

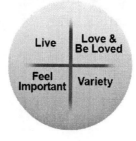

1. To live
2. To love and be loved
3. To feel important, to have value and significance
4. To have variety

The most interesting one to me, by the way, is the fact that we all have a need for variety. That's why you have a closet full of different kinds of clothes, you go on vacations, and you pay for cable or satellite TV to watch a wide variety of shows and productions. We have a very strong need for variety.

We represent the first piece of our model with a wheel, because this is the wheel that drives the model. It gives power to the model. You may even label this wheel with the word "engine," because this is where the model gets its power.

Belief Window:

The second piece of the model looks like a window. Up on top of that window are the words "Belief Window." Inside of that window is the word "principles."

Belief Window

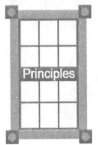

Understand this fact. You have what I like to call a Belief Window. It sits in front of your face. A wire comes from the back of your head across the top and hooks onto that window. Every time you move, it goes with you. You look out into the world through this window. You accept information from the world in through this window. On this window you have placed thousands of principles that you have accepted as correct principles.

The minute I say the word 'principles', a lot of people start thinking about heavy-duty religious stuff. It's true, that religious and ethical principles may be on your Belief Window, but there are thousands of little tiny principles as well. We put principles on our Belief Window because we believe they'll help us satisfy those four needs. The number of principles you have on your Belief Window is a function of your age. The older you are, the more principles on your Belief Window.

An example of a principle you might have on your Belief Window, might go something like this: "All Doberman Pinschers are vicious."

Which of the four needs is driving this principle? It clearly has something to do with the need to live. Somewhere in our life, we have decided to accept the idea that Doberman Pinschers are vicious as a correct principle. We believe it, so we put that principle on our Belief Window.

If Then Rules:

The third piece of the model looks like a little bridge. On top of that bridge is the word, "rules." Inside of that bridge are two tiny words: "if" and "then."

This is how the Belief Window works: The minute you put a principle on your Belief Window, you immediately start to create rules that will govern your behavior, based on the principle on your Belief Window. This all goes on in your head at the speed of lightning. You do it automatically and sometimes even without realizing which principles you are actually putting on your Belief Window.

We call these "If-Then Rules." So let us say that you do have the principle on your Belief Window that all Doberman Pinschers are vicious. You have accepted this as a correct principle. So when you encounter a big Doberman pinscher, what will you do? You will leap tall buildings with a single bound. You will run, you will evade. You will have a very specific set of rules all set up based on that principle on your Belief Window.

Now understand this fact: The first three pieces of this model are all invisible. You can't see the process. No one else can see it. But it's going on every second you breathe.

Behavior Patterns:

Let's go to the fourth piece now. The fourth piece of the Reality Model looks like a triangle on its side. Down the slope on the top of that triangle are the words " behavior patterns." Inside of that triangle is the word "action."

Let's go back to that same principle, all Doberman Pinschers are vicious. If that's true then we set up our rules. Rules are automatic: If you go in somebody's yard and there's a big dog, what behavior pattern will we see? You will do the same action every single time.

Let's take another principle through the model to this point. Here is a principle: "My self-worth is dependent on my possessions." Do you know anyone that has that principle on his or her Belief Window? Which of the four needs would drive this principle? To feel important for sure. Anything else?

Let's pretend I have a second principle on my belief window: European possessions are better. So I have two principles on my Belief Window: (1) My self-worth is dependent on my stuff, and (2) European stuff is better.

Let's take that through the model. If that's true, then I set up my rules. Rules are automatic. It's now time for me to buy a car. What kind of car will I buy? What kind of clothes will I wear? European, of course. And I am likely not going to feel good about myself without that car, or those clothes.

Let me tell you a story to illustrate how Belief Windows can be passed on from generation to generation. A man comes into his kitchen on Sunday morning and notices his wife is cooking a wonderful Sunday dinner. As she pulls from the oven a beautifully cooked ham, he notices that the ends have been removed from the ham. He was curious by that. He asked his wife, "Why did you cut the ends off the ham?"

She said, "It makes it tastes better."

"How do you know that?"

"My mother told me that."

So on this woman's Belief Window is the principle that if you cut the ends off the ham it makes it taste better.

Now the man is really curious because he never saw his own mother do that. The next Sunday he's at the in-laws' house for dinner. He took his mother-in-law aside and said, "I understand you cut the ends off your ham."

"I do."

"Why do you do that?"

24

"It makes it tastes better."

"How do you know that?"

"My mother told me that."

Two generations of women now have the principle on their Belief Window: cutting the ends off the ham makes it taste better. He didn't understand that logic. The grandmother was still alive at 93 years old. She lived in Texas. He called her up on the phone.

"I understand you cut the ends off your ham."

"I do."

"Why do you do that?"

"Won't fit in the oven if I don't."

Two generations later, the principle or belief floats down on a Belief Window: cutting the ends off the ham makes it taste better.

Results and Feedback

Look at the last piece of the model. The final piece in the model is a little box. Inside the box is the word "results."

Results

Results allow us to examine current principles on our Belief Window. If we don't like the results we are getting, **we can move through the model to see what principles on our Belief Window are causing these results.** There is a line labeled Feedback connecting the results box with the Needs wheel. Results are linked with the needs that everyone has. Whatever behavior we exhibit, it is ultimately an attempt to fulfill one or more of those needs. The results of that behavior will determine whether or not we have successfully met our Needs.

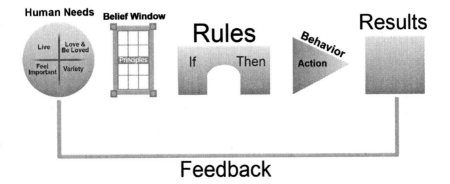

Needs and Natural Laws

I am now going to introduce you to seven natural laws. If you will commit these seven laws to memory, the impact on your personal and professional decision making process will amaze you. Let's look at the first two natural laws and then run some principles through the model.

First Natural Law: If the results of your behavior do not meet your needs, there is an incorrect principle or belief on your Belief Window.

Second Natural Law. Results take time to measure.

Let's say there is a person named Gary. Gary has a principle on his Belief Window: "My self-worth is dependent on never losing an argument". If that's true then he sets up his rules. Rules are automatic. He gets in an argument with his 15-year-old son. What behavior pattern will we see? He will make sure that he wins every single time due to his belief that his self-worth is dependent on never losing an argument.

Now ask this question: will the results of Gary's behavior meet his needs over time? Yes or no? If the answer is no, what does that mean about his Belief Window? It means that there is a negative, and/or incorrect or incomplete principle on his Belief Window.

I'm going to give you another principle now, let's take it all the way through the model. Here is a principle: 'My self-worth is dependent on never losing at games'. Do you know anyone who has that principle on his or her Belief Window?

Let's pretend that I have that belief on my Belief Window. My self-worth is dependent on never losing at games. Which of the four needs is driving that belief? "Feeling important," for sure. If that principle is true, then I set up my rules: I'm not okay unless I win.

I now get in a game with someone, and I start to lose. What behavior pattern will you see from me?

I'll cheat.

And I'll do everything in my power to win. Now we've got to ask the question: Will the results of my behavior meet my needs over time? If the answer is no, what does that mean about my Belief Window? Is there an incorrect principle on my Belief Window?

Several years ago, on the front page of USA Today, it read in big letters that 1 out of 3 CEOs cheat at golf. It was a big article. It told how they did it. So the reader now has to ask: If they'll fudge in a $10 game of golf, what will they do in a million-dollar deal? This was right around the time Enron collapsed. What do you think was on the Belief Window of the people at Enron?

Okay, I'm going to walk a potentially controversial principle through the model. For the sake of discussion only, let's say that a person has the principle on their belief window that men are better than women. Do you know any men who have that principle on their Belief Windows? Do you know any women who have a similar belief on their Belief Windows? Which of the four needs would drive a principle like that? Survival? To feel important?

That actually was a prevalent belief in the world until about 100 years ago. As a side note, one of the first debates Benjamin Franklin took part in as a young man was in defense of educating women in this country.

Franklin shares in his autobiography: "John Collins was of the Opinion that it (educating women) was improper; and that they were naturally unequal to it. I took the contrary Side"

All right, let's continue through the model. I have the principle on my Belief Window that men are better than women. Saturday morning my wife says, "Hyrum, I have a lot of errands to run today, would you mind vacuuming the house while I'm gone?" Given what I believe, what behavior will you see from me? I might say, "I don't do that, that's women's work;"

Now we have to ask the question, will the results of my behavior meet my needs over time? Probably not. So what do we know about my Belief Window? I've got an incorrect principle on my Belief Window.

Where do we get principles for our Belief Windows? Where do they come from? Well, they start when we're pretty small. If a little girl in our society acts like a little boy, what do we call her? A tomboy. That is okay in our culture. If a little boy acts like a little girl, what do we call him? We call him a sissy. That's the nicest thing we call him. That's not okay in our culture.

A ten-year-old boy comes into his garage Saturday morning. While doing what kids do in a garage on Saturday morning, he accidentally tips a box off the shelf and it lands on his foot. It smashes three toes, he bleeds all over the floor, and he starts to cry. Dad comes into the garage. What does Dad say to that little boy?

"Don't cry. Men don't cry."

"This hurts, I'd like to cry. Why can't I cry, Dad?"

"Because men don't cry."

Scientists tell us that tears exuded over an onion have a very different chemistry than tears exuded in anguish. We apparently get rid of some ugly toxins from our bodies when we cry. We don't allow men that privilege in our culture. "Real" men don't cry.

Changing Principles and Beliefs Changes Behavior

Before any of my behavior will change, the principle on my Belief Window has to change, or the behavior will never change. I have to find an alternative principle. What principle will likely work? Men and women are equal. They are different, wonderfully different, but equal.

If I get that principle on my Belief Window, will it alter my behavior? Yes it will. Now on a Saturday morning my wife says, "Hyrum, I've got a lot of errands to run today, would you mind vacuuming the house while I'm gone?" What kind of behavior do you think we will see next? "Love to do it."

Not only do individuals have Belief Windows, groups have Belief Windows as well. Families have them, neighborhoods have them, cities have them, corporations have them, and nations have them.

I'm going to give you a principle now that we at Franklin had on our corporate Belief Window in the beginning. I say, "had" because we discovered that this was not a good principle. Ask yourselves what the need was driving this principle, and let's take it through the model. Here was our principle: 'Cut costs no matter what.'

That doesn't sound like a bad principle, does it? Which of the four needs is in play? To live, or sometimes it felt like survival was driving it. Why would the needs of a corporation be identical to the needs of a human being? Corporations are made up of human beings.

So the principle on our Belief Window was 'cut costs no matter what'. If that's true, then we set up our rules. Now, nobody sends a memo out saying, "Set your rules up". Rules are automatic. It's now time for us to hire a receptionist. What kind of receptionist will we hire? Based on our principle, we will hire the cheapest one we can find. Will the results of that behavior meet our needs over time as a firm?

Three weeks later, a senior vice president from one of our biggest clients, called me on the phone.

"Hyrum, you have a really interesting receptionist."

"Really?"

"Yeah. She doesn't speak English."

"She doesn't?"

He said, "No. I called in and asked for some things and she said, "We ain't got none o' them, Jack.""

We learned something that day. Who is our window to the corporate world if not our receptionist? We were by then managing our little firm with this Reality Model. We sat down and asked ourselves, "What principle on our corporate Belief Window allowed us to hire somebody like that?" We came up with it pretty fast. 'Cut costs, no matter what.' We decided we didn't like that principle, so we took it off our Belief Window, and put a new one on.

The new principle we put on our Belief Window was this: 'We want the finest reputation in America.' A new principle on a Belief Window requires a new set of rules. Rules are automatic. We clearly needed a new receptionist. What kind of receptionist were we going to hire now? The highest paid, finest receptionist in the state.

Now this was a very interesting experience for me. The person we selected to be our new receptionist was already at a director level in our little firm. There were only about 400 of us then. Her name was Linda. I called her into my office. I was excited.

I said, "Linda, there's a new role we want you to play here at the firm. We want you to be our receptionist."

What do you think she said? "Why don't you just fire me, Hyrum?"

What was on her Belief Window about receptionists? She thought they were all airheads. We had to get a new principle on her Belief Window. We walked her through this whole process on how we arrived at her as our new receptionist. We gave her a raise. She got a new principle on her Belief Window. She took the job, and became responsible for 18 other people in our new external communications department. It all started by getting a new principle on our corporate Belief Window.

I would like to share with you an eye-opening experience that will help you understand how powerful this simple model can be. One day I was sitting in my office, which in those days was rare. The phone rang and I picked it up. It was the U.S. Attorney for the District of Utah, which happens to be the entire state of Utah.

He said, "Hyrum, I am sick and tired of locking kids up in this state for drug and alcohol abuse. I've decided to go to every high school in the state. We are going to put on a big assembly. I've got the Utah Jazz basketball team willing to send a player with us and we're going to talk these kids out of drugs and alcohol." He said, "Would you go with us and do a thirty to forty-minute talk and teach these kids how to get control of their lives?"

I got pretty excited about that. I said, "Let's go for it."

We went to 148 schools in Utah and twenty schools outside the state.

Halfway through this experience we discovered that we were wasting our time in the high schools. Why? The average age for starting drugs and alcohol in the state of Utah is twelve. So we started going to elementary and middle schools.

One day, we went to another high school. The name of the high school is not important, but what happened there is very important. On this particular day, the U.S. Attorney was not able to go. He had to be in Washington for some reason, and so he sent one of his Assistant U.S. Attorneys, a man named Sam. The Utah Jazz basketball team was on a road trip somewhere so they could not send one of their players. So just Sam and I went.

We walked into this high school. The principal met us in the lobby, took us into his office, sat us down and said,

"You guys are accustomed to talking to the whole student body, right?"

I said, "Yes, we usually talk to the whole student body."

"I don't want you to talk to the whole student body, they're not the ones with the problem. I want you to talk to my druggies and alcoholics."

"Do you know who they are?"

"Of course, I know who they are."

"Hey, we'll talk to anybody you want."

"Great."

He took us down to a band room. It had a graduated floor and there was only one door in the room. Sam and I walked through the door, sat down and waited for the bell to ring. The bell rang, the door opened, and in through that door came 50 of the hardest looking kids I have ever seen. I've talked to over 400,000 kids. I know what a hard kid looks like. Many of them had hair hanging below their shoulders. Several of them had earrings in places on their faces you would not believe. They had tattoos and studded belts with chains hanging off them. These kids were ugly. They came in and draped themselves across the chairs in this room.

As they sat down waiting for the bell to ring, they looked around and recognized each other. And when they recognized each other, the hostility in the room went nuts.

The bell rang again, the door opened and the principal walked to the front of the room. Before he could open his mouth, one kid jumped out of his chair, accosted the principal and said, "Hey, how come we're in here anyway?"

34

The principal said, "Because you're all druggies and alcoholics, and these two guys are going to fix it." Then the principal turned around and walked out. I've had many introductions in my career, but this was the most interesting.

While the principal had been talking, I'd been looking at this kid and had picked him out as the ringleader of the group. Longhaired, five piercings in his face and a big studded chain hanging off his arm.

Sam was assigned to talk first. Now Sam is a wonderful guy. Putting people in jail is what he does for a living and he's very good at it. Talking to young people was really not his thing, and this became evident really fast. Sam got up. As he took those three steps to the front of the room, for some reason he felt like he needed to look more like those kids looked. So he tore off his jacket, took his tie off, threw them on a chair in the front row, and said, "I'll tell you what, guys, if I catch you dealing drugs, I will lock you up and throw the key away. Have you got that? I will lock you up."

The kid who had accosted the principal jumped out of his chair a second time: "The heck you will, Jack." He didn't say "heck". I learned some new words that day.

"We're minors. We're under 18 and you can't touch us."

Then the entire class joined in, "That's right, baby, you can't touch us."

They were right. And Sam was done. He walked back and sat down. He was supposed to talk fifteen minutes he talked for ninety seconds. He sat next to me, leaned over and said, "You can have this mob."

I got up and walked to the front of the room. I said to myself as I took those three steps, "You know, Hyrum, there is no way this can get any worse." It got worse.

I got to the front of the room. There was a kid about halfway back. He was longhaired and his shirt was open to his navel. He was draped across two chairs and had tattoos everywhere. He was wearing these funky glasses. This kid was feeling no pain whatsoever. For some reason I took him on.

I said, "Well, it looks like we have our class nerd here."

He jumped out of his chair, took his glasses off: "I don't have to take that."

I said, "That's right, you don't. Why don't you get out?"

"Okay, I will," and stormed over to the door. He turned around and swore at me using three words I really never had heard before, and slammed the door. When he slammed the door, the entire class piped up almost in unison: "Hey man, let's get the guy with the suit!" That's how it started.

Normally, when we'd go to a high school we'd have 1,500 kids in a big auditorium. We'd show a film on kids who got messed up in Salt Lake City on drugs. Then one of the Jazz players would get up and talk about drugs in athletics, and then the U.S. Attorney would talk, and then I'd get up and do a thirty-five to forty minute thing on how

36

to gain control of your life. And I would teach them a Shakespeare poem.

But I found myself saying to myself, "Hyrum, if you try and teach these kids a Shakespeare poem, today is your last day on the planet, friend. You had better do something else."

Up to this point, I had never tried to teach the Reality Model to a group of young people and certainly not this kind of young people. But I found myself up there saying to myself, "You know what, these kids are going to learn that model if it kills me." I wasn't sure it wouldn't at that point.

So I said, "All right, listen up. I came down here to teach you a model. It's called the Reality Model. You're going to burn it into your brains before you walk out that door. I don't have a blackboard up here so I need five volunteers. I'll pick the volunteers. You, get down here." I dragged a longhaired kid up, sat him in a chair.

"You're my Needs wheel. There are four needs. Commit them to memory: To live, To love and be loved, To feel important, Variety. Give me one back." He couldn't give me one back. Finally, I got him to mutter one.

Then I picked the kid who'd been accosting everybody to be my Belief Window. It took me six minutes to get his real name. He gave me 11 wrong names. I finally got his real name. JD. I brought him up front, "You're my Belief Window." I finally had five kids up there, all representing a piece of the model.

I said, "Okay, I'm going to give you a principle you might have on your Belief Window. You give me the need driving that, and let's take it through the model. Here's the principle: My self-worth is dependent on being okay with my friends."

Do you know any young people that have that principle on their belief window? Do you know any old people that have that principle on their Belief Window?

I said, "Give me the Need driving that."

A kid popped up: "To feel important."

I said, "Yeah, probably that. How about to be loved? Let's take that through the model. If that's true, then you set up your rules. You go to a party. Some of your friends offer you drugs and alcohol, what are you going to do?"

The whole class chimed in, "Hey man, we're going to take it."

"That's right, you're going to take it. Will the results of that behavior meet your needs over time?"

They didn't have the foggiest idea what I was talking about.

Identifying Correct Principles

So we started driving stuff through the model. Twenty-five minutes into this class, JD, the kid who had been my Belief Window, figured out the model.

He suddenly jumped out of his chair, "Okay, Hyrum."

When JD jumped out of his chair, the class went stone quiet. You could hear a pin drop. You could see in their faces the thought, "Holy #&*%@#! JD is going to get the guy with the suit!"

He said, "Let me tell you how stupid this model is. You just told us if the results of our behavior don't meet our needs, there's an incorrect principle on our Belief Window, right?"

I was excited. He used the words perfectly. I said, "Right."

I knew exactly where he was going, so I stopped him and said, "Wait a minute, JD, do you drink?"

"Yeah, I drink."

"How much do you drink?"

"Eight or ten beers a week. I get smashed on weekends."

"You get smashed every weekend?"

"Yeah."

"Are you an alcoholic?"

"No way, man, you can't be an alcoholic drinking like that."

"You just gave me a principle on your belief window."

"I did?"

"Yeah, you did. You just told me you believe you can take eight beers a week, get smashed on weekends and you won't be an alcoholic. You told me you believe that."

"So?"

"That's all, JD, just want to make sure you understand. Go ahead."

Then he said, "Okay, Hyrum, that means if the results of our behavior do meet our needs, there's a correct principle on our Belief Window, right?"

"Right."

"Okay, Hyrum, I have a principle on my Belief Window."

I was excited. He was using the model perfectly.

He said, "I don't care what those kids think about me. The principle on my belief window is that drugs and alcohol are fun. And the need driving that. Variety baby! Take that through your stupid model. If that's true, then I set up my rules. I go to a party and my friends offer me drugs and alcohol, so I take it. Do the results of that meet my needs? You bet it does, man. When I take drugs and alcohol, I feel terrific. That means I've got a correct principle on my Belief Window, right?"

You could hear a pin drop. I stood there for a second and said, "Right."

And he said, "Right?"

And I said, "Yeah, right. But you forgot the second law, JD. **Results take time to measure.** You don't know yet. You may feel good that night, or over the weekend, but over time, is that going to meet your needs?"

He came back with lightning speed, "Okay, okay, man, that means I take drugs and alcohol all my life and prove it, right?"

Pretty smart kid. I said, "Yeah, you can do that. That's the dumbest way to find out if you've got a good principle on your Belief Window, but you can do that if you want."

"How else are you going to do it?"

I said, "It's called seeds and fruits."

"What does that mean?"

I said, "That means you take a look at somebody else's life that took drugs and alcohol all their lives and see if it really met their needs. Can we do that?"

"Yeah."

I said, "Okay, JD, you give me one example."

Now at that point we were nose to nose in front of the class. I was dripping wet, but they didn't know. I kept my coat on.

"You give me one example of somebody who took drugs and alcohol all their lives where it really met their needs. One example."

Do you know what example he gave me? Elvis Presley.

"Elvis Presley?" I said. "Where's Presley, for crying out loud?"

"Dead."

"How come?"

"OD'd on drugs."

"Did that meet his needs?"

JD sat down. I addressed the class. "Give me another example."

The second example they threw at me was Janis Joplin.

"Where's Janis Joplin?"

"Dead."

"How come?"

"OD'd on drugs."

"Did that meet her needs?"

The third example, and I am not kidding, was John Belushi.

"Where's Belushi?"

"Dead."

"How come?"

"OD'd on drugs."

"Did that meet his needs?"

For the first time, I had their undivided attention. You could hear a pin drop.

"Now listen, folks. I did not come down here to tell you what belongs on your Belief Window. That is none of my business. I came down here to tell you that you've got a Belief Window. You've got the same four needs I've got. And you're putting principles and beliefs on that window every day that you think are going to meet your needs. Are you mature enough to take that window off, put it on the table and find out if those principles are correct?"

There was a kid with green hair that jumped out of his chair at this point and said, "This is a bunch of garbage!"

"What do you mean this is a bunch of garbage?"

"Yeah, who cares about this stupid model? We're all going to be dead in ten years anyway."

"What do you mean you're going to be dead in ten years?"

"Yeah, we're going to blow ourselves up."

"You just gave me a principle on your Belief Window."

"I did?"

"Yeah you did.

You just told me that you believe you'll be dead in ten years. How many of you believe that?"

Forty-three hands went up. I said, "Let's take that one through the model. We will be dead in ten years. If that's true then, and it's now time for you to perform in school how are you going to perform in school?"

The kid sitting next to him jumped out of his chair and said, "This is the dumbest kid in school, man, he's flunking out."

I said, "Flunking out. Are the results of that going to meet your needs over time? Suppose you're not dead in ten years. Twelve years from today, you're still alive. Who's going to buy the green dye for your hair, for crying out loud?"

I wish I had a picture of this kid. It looked like he had been hit by a baseball bat.

He stood there and said, "That doesn't mean you don't try."

"The heck it doesn't. How are you doing in school? Right now, how are you doing in school?"

The kid sitting next to him jumped up again, "This is the village idiot, man, he's flunking out."

I said, "You got many friends like him?"

The bell rang. The door opened and the principal came back: "Your time's up."

I said, "Well, I guess our time's up."

Two kids jumped up: "No way, man, we're not done."

"We're not done? Do you want some more?" I asked.

"We've got to have another hour."

"Can't have another hour, its lunchtime," the principal announced.

"Well, can we come back after lunch?" I asked.

"I guess you can," said the principal.

"Be back in your seats at 12:15."

Behavior Patterns Identify Results

At five minutes past twelve, sixty kids came back. Ten uglier than the first fifty. The five kids that I had up front were back in their chairs before anyone else arrived. They wanted those chairs. When they all came back, a lot of the hostility was gone but we weren't friends yet. I decided that I was going to try something anyway.

"I need to make a very important point here. When you witness a pattern of behavior, can you tell what's on the Belief Window? Pretty much, yes, you can. More scary than that, if you know what's on someone's Belief Window, what can you predict with great accuracy? You can predict their behavior and ultimately their results. Now I had made that point to this class before lunch. So I brought the ten who had missed the first hour up to speed.

I said, "Okay guys, remember I said that when you witness a pattern of behavior, you can tell what's on the Belief Window, right?"

"Yeah, that's right."

"I'm witnessing a pattern of behavior today."

They all looked at me: "What are you talking about?"

"You people look awful."

The anger and hostility returned pretty fast.

I said, "Look at you people. You try and run in the world I run in, you wouldn't last 30 seconds. You look horrible." Then I picked a kid out: "You, stand up." This kid stood up. He had the most beautiful long hair I had ever seen, down below his shoulders. I would kill for hair like that. "You're wearing long hair."

"So?"

"How long have you been wearing long hair?"

"Five years."

"That makes that a pattern of behavior, right?"

"Yeah."

"Well I want to know what's on your Belief Window driving you to wear long hair."

Unmet Needs Drive Behavior

This kid stood there for a full minute. Do you have any idea how long a minute is, when you're about to die? At the end of the minute, he stood there and said, "It gets my father's attention."

Which of the four Needs was not being met? "To Love and be loved."

Understand, that when any of these needs are not being met, all of our energy flows to meet that need, automatically. And we start putting principles on our Belief Window with lightning speed that we think will meet that need. If we put a principle on our Belief Window that drives behavior that works short term and destroys long term, will we still do it? Tragically, most of us will, unless we choose to take control of this thing.

I wanted to win these kids back, because they were all madder than heck at me. I said, "Now listen, guys, when I walked in here today, you saw a pattern of my behavior, did you not?"

"What are you talking about, man?"

"Didn't I throw a long-haired kid out of here?"

"Yeah, you did."

"Well, maybe I have something on my Belief Window."

A kid jumped up: "You think all long-haired kids are rotten."

"Well I don't think I believe that, but let's say I do believe that, let's put that on my window. All long-haired kids are rotten. If that's true then, I come to your school and a long-haired kid gives me a hard time, what am I going to do?"

The whole class roared, "You're going to throw him out! "Right, I threw him out. Will the results of my behavior meet my needs over time?" Sixty heads in the room nodded up and down.

I said, "No, no, no. Is that kid here?"

"No."

"Is he getting the benefit of this class?"

"No".

"Will he ever speak to me again?"

"No".

"Is that meeting my needs?"

"No!"

Another kid popped up, "You got a screwed up Belief Window, Hyrum!"

They were starting to get it.

JD jumped out of his chair. By this time JD and I had become friends. He said, "Okay, Hyrum, there are two things we got to run through our model". He actually said 'our' model. I wanted to hug him.

He continued, "First of all, why did you come down here? Why are you at our school today?"

I said, "Because I have something on my Belief Window."

"What is it?"

"Well, I have the principle on my Belief Window, that I'm supposed to make a difference."

"What does that mean?"

"I don't know what that means. I heard Winston Churchill give a speech before he died. The man said that he was going to make a difference. So I decided Hyrum's going to make a difference too. Which of the four needs would drive that?"

A new kid popped up: "To feel important."

I said, "Yeah, and how about to love? Why would I come talk to a sick group like you, variety, trust me." Then I said, "Let's take that through the model. If that's true then, and your school asks me to come talk to you about drugs and alcohol, what am I going to do?"

The whole class: "You're going to do it."

A kid popped up: "Well, Hyrum, is it meeting your needs?"

I said, "I don't know. Remember, it takes time to measure results. I don't know yet."

JD said, "Okay, all right, I understand that. Now here's the real thing." When he started talking about the real thing, he was pacing back and forth in front of the room.

"There's this girl, she's my friend. She is not my girlfriend."

The minute he started talking about this girl, the class went deathly quiet. They all knew which girl he was talking about.

"She's a cocaine addict, and an alcoholic. Her parents are alcoholics and cocaine addicts. They beat her all the time. They're the most screwed up people you've ever seen. She's going to kill herself today. She called me this morning and she said that she's taking herself out today. How are we going to keep this girl from committing suicide?"

They all expected a golden answer from the guy with the suit. I stood there for a minute and said, "I don't know."

"What do you mean you don't know?"

"How am I supposed to know?"

"You've got a suit, you're supposed to know!" I thought that that was an interesting belief on their Belief Window.

"Well I don't know," I said. "Let's put what we know in the model. What is her behavior?"

JD, "I told you, she's a cocaine addict and an alcoholic."

I said, "Will the results of her behavior meet her needs over time?"

I then had the most electric teaching experience I have ever had. Sixty heads in that room shook their heads from side to side.

I said, "You've got that right. What does that mean?"

A kid stood up, "She's got a screwed up Belief Window!"

JD shouted, "If I go tell her she's got a screwed up Belief Window, she'll throw me out."

I said, "Guys, it's deeper than a Belief Window. There's a need not being met. Which of the four needs aren't being met?"

Another kid wearing an army field jacket and long hair stood up. He looked like he'd just had a revelation. This kid looked at me like I was a complete idiot and said, "Nobody loves her."

I replied, "What are we going to do about that?"

The same kid, dumbfounded, looked at me and he said, "We love her, dummy."

"And how are we going to do that?"

These kids then came up with the most wonderful ideas on how they could show that girl they loved her.

I said, "Do you think if we started showing her we loved her, we could start talking to her about principles on Belief Windows?"

"Yeah."

The bell rang again. The principal came back to tell us the time was really up. He threw everybody out. JD lingered behind.

He walked up to me and got right up in my face. "Let me tell you something. I've been in drug and alcohol therapy for ten years."

JD was sixteen years old his brother had given him cocaine when he was six.

He said, "I've been in jail four times, I've had every shrink in this state try and figure me out. This is the first time anything made any sense to me."

I stayed right there, nose to nose, "JD, I'm going to tell you this one more time. I did not come down here to tell you what belongs on your Belief Window. That is none of my business. I came down here to tell you that you've got a Belief Window. You've got the same needs I've got and you're putting principles on that window every day that you think will meet your needs. Are you man enough to put that Belief Window on the table and find out what's incorrect?"

JD responded, "Yeah, I am."

"Well, I guess we'll see, won't we?"

Understanding Behavioral Responsibility

Here are two powerful facts about the model:

- It places responsibility for behavior right smack on the human being where it belongs. I give this as my opinion. There arrives a point in our lives when we must take total responsibility for our behavior. Do you buy that?

- You can be very confronting about attacking somebody's Belief Window, because you're not attacking the person, you're attacking the behavior. You're attacking something they can fix. "I'm okay, Dad, right?" "I love you a lot, kid, but you've got a screwed-up Belief Window, and we are going to do surgery on it."

Growth Requires Changing Principles

Third Natural Law: Growth is the process of changing principles on your Belief Window.

Corporate America spends $80 billion dollars a year training their people. Why? Why do corporations send their people to seminars and training? To make them perform better and help them improve their behavior, right?

At a large investment firm where we trained a lot of people in time management, I shared the model with a senior training manager. She got pretty excited about it.

She said, "Hyrum, all the training we do here is designed to improve, better, and enhance the behavior and productivity of our people, right?"

I said, "Right, that's probably why you do the training."

"That means, Hyrum, that what we're really doing, is trying to get new and better principles on their Belief Windows so they can govern themselves."

She was right. If you go to a class or seminar at a corporation or in public, "The facilitator should say: 'The principle we'd like you to have on your Belief Window as a result of this class today is---,' and then lay it out. That is really the message we want people to understand."

Unmet Needs Lead To Addiction

Fourth Natural Law: Addiction is the result of deep and unmet needs.

Why do young people do a lot of the dumb things they do? They're trying to meet needs, powerful, compelling, and driving needs. Why do adults do a lot of the dumb stuff they do? Same reason. If we put principles on our Belief Windows that drive behavior that works short term and destroys long term, will we still do it? Many of us will, unless we choose to take control.

Importance of Self-Worth

Fifth Natural Law: If your self-worth is dependent on anything external, you are in big trouble.

We get some very interesting things on our Belief Windows. I'm going to share a couple of principles with you now, and this time I want you to predict the behavior these principles will drive.

Here is a principle: 'My self-worth is dependent on the size of my waist.' Do you know anyone who has that principle on his or her Belief Window? What's the extreme behavior that principle could drive? Possibly eating disorders, etc.? My kids went to high school in a suburban community. Every morning at 5:30 fifty young women would show up at the high school for the rehearsal of a nationally ranked women's drill team. They weighed every young woman every morning. One pound overweight and they were thrown off the team. They don't do that anymore, but there were nine anorexic students on that team. Do you see where this comes from?

Here's a principle a lot of men in our culture have: 'My self-worth is dependent on my job and it has to be a white-collar job.' The fact that I am magnificent with my hands doesn't matter. Somewhere I've picked up that I've got to carry a briefcase like everybody else in my high school class.

Many years ago I was in Boston. Sitting on the front row was an attorney. How did I know he was an attorney, he told me. He also told me why he was an attorney. He was the fifth generation of attorneys in his family in Boston. If you were a male baby in his home, you were destined to be an attorney.

He hated being an attorney.

Two weeks after he went through the Reality Model he delicately approached his wife and said, "My needs are not being met by being an attorney. I hate being an attorney."

He was forty-nine years old, with a big six-figure income. "Do you know what I want to do? I want to teach music at Boston College."

What do you think his wife said? "Have you lost your mind?"

He said, "If I make this major career change at this point in my life, will you still love me?"

"Of course, I'll love you...I'll miss you."

This fellow made the change. He is now teaching music at Boston College. He cut his income by a factor of eight and he is happier than he's ever been before. Is that possible? We get some really weird things on our Belief Windows about money, don't we?

By the way, his wife stayed with him.

Experiencing Inner Peace

Sixth Natural Law: When the results of your behavior do meet your needs over time, you experience inner peace.

The central theme of the seminar we used to teach at Franklin Quest was the acquisition and maintenance of inner peace. People were stunned to hear that in a corporate seminar. I'd be teaching a class and about an hour into it somebody would raise their hand and say, "Aren't you going to teach us how to make a list?"

"Would you like to know how to make a list?"

"Well, yeah."

"I'll teach you how to make a list but that's not why you're here."

"It's not?"

"No."

"Why am I here?"

"You're here to get inner peace."

"Oh. Are you going to give me a planner?"

"Would you like a planner?"

"Yeah."

"I'll give you a planner but that's not why you're here."

"It's not?"

"No."

"Why am I here?"

"You're here to get inner peace."

"Oh." By the time we finished, they got it.

Would you like to have an eight-hour time management seminar in nine seconds?

Find out what matters most to you. Bring the events of your life in line with what matters most to you, and you have a right to inner peace.

That's all we taught. This is a 6,000 year-old idea. It's really true, by the way. That's how inner peace comes. By the way you owe me $295.00 for that eight-hour seminar.

Harmonizing the Mind

Seventh Natural Law: The mind naturally seeks harmony when presented with two opposing principles.

Psychologists call this cognitive dissonance. We tend to go to the principle that's going to work. Let's go back to the marriage example. We presented two principles: men are better than women, and men and women are equal. Which one will I likely pick? I'm going to pick the one that's going to work. But, suppose I choose not to change that principle on my Belief Window and I stick to 'men are better than women'. I show up at work tomorrow and my new boss is a woman. Do I have a problem? Has she got a problem? (Short term)

Understand that this entire model is nothing more than a visual representation of what's going on anyway. Its power is in its simplicity.

There's not a person in the world that doesn't have those four needs. You've got them. You've got Belief Windows and they are covered with principles. Some are good and frankly some may not be. You've got rules all set up that are driving your behavior based on what you believe to be true. Where it breaks down is that we tend not to measure the results. So there's pain and we're not sure why.

North Philadelphia is one of the most dangerous communities in America. There are killings almost every night. We at Franklin Quest adopted a high school in the middle of North Philadelphia. The Ben Franklin High School. Years ago the principal, Dr. Norman Spencer, an amazing man, invited me to come speak to the juniors and seniors at Ben Franklin High School. They would not allow me to drive myself into the neighborhood. It was that dangerous. Taxicabs didn't go into that neighborhood. So I was escorted in by two police squad cars. I watched them lock the doors on the inside of a four-story high school with chains at 8:30 in the morning.

I asked Dr. Spencer: "Why are you locking your doors with chains?"

"Well, that's the only way we can keep the drug pushers out of the high school."

"Oh."

Then we went into an auditorium. There were 900 black kids. I was the only white person in about 32 blocks. If you want a sobering experience, fly to Philadelphia, rent a car, and drive into North Philadelphia. You will think you've driven into Berlin two days after the Second World War. It's that tough.

I spent 90 minutes with those kids. I taught them the model. I had the Belief Window projected on a big screen. About an hour into it, I walked out into the auditorium and confronted a kid sitting in the aisle. As I walked up to him, he stood up to confront me. I got right up in his face and said, "Suppose you lived in a neighborhood where on the neighborhood Belief Window was the principle: 'All blacks are stupid.'

It got really quiet. This kid stood there and said: "All blacks aren't stupid."

"I didn't say they were. I said suppose you lived in a neighborhood where on the neighborhood Belief Window was the principle: 'All blacks are stupid.'

"All blacks aren't stupid!"

It took me four times. When he finally realized what I was doing he looked at me and he said, "I live in a neighborhood like that."

"How much fun is that?"

"It's no fun."

From this experience we see how an engrained and seemingly simple belief can have huge consequences for an individual, a family, a city, and a culture. The results of this belief are shown through what the individuals, families, and culture do. Sometimes the beliefs are good, and sometimes they are bad.

Pre-judgments and Prejudices

All of our pre-judgments or prejudices are principles on Belief Windows, are they not? All blacks are.... all Hispanics are.... all rich people are.... all poor people are.... Etc. Etc. Those principles can drive some very painful behavior, can they not? If that behavior is ever going to change, what has to change first? The principle on the Belief Window has to change first or the behavior will never change. Maybe all blacks aren't, maybe all Hispanics aren't, etc.

I grew up in Honolulu. I spent my first 18 years in Hawaii. It never occurred to me to be prejudiced. I was one of five white kids in a class of 60 non-white kids. I had to come to Los Angeles to discover that prejudice is alive and well in this the U.S.

You have learned the model and the 7 Natural Laws that make it work. In order to make changes in a Belief Window that is causing negative results, it is necessary to learn how to apply the model.

Chapter 3
Steps to Using the Model

In the last sections we learned the power of this model from the High School kids who were druggies and alcoholics. The goal of this section is for you to learn in depth the steps on how to use the model in your own life and to be able to teach it to someone else.

Let me introduce you to the six steps on how to use this model in a very simple but powerful way.

Step 1. Identify The Behavior Patterns

Why do you suppose we start with behavior? Take a look at the model again.

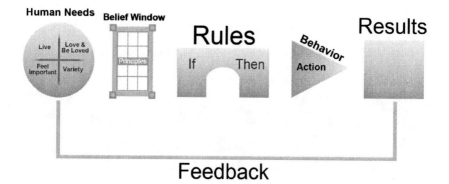

What's the only visible piece in the model? Behavior. That's where you have to start.

For about four years, every six months I'd visit a place in Utah called the Point of the Mountain. It is the state penitentiary.

The first time I was there, I was given 90 inmates in blue uniforms. We were in a cafeteria in the basement of this big prison. I had my Reality Model up on the blackboard. We were about 90 minutes into it, and I said, "Okay guys, you exhibited some behavior that got you in this place, right?"

"Yeah, that's right."

"Is that behavior going to meet your needs over time? Do you guys want to talk about time?" They did not want to talk about time. I said, "If you people get out of here, what's the probability of your coming back?"

"Oh, we all come back."

"Right, you all come back, which means what didn't change?"

"Our behavior."

"Of course, your behavior didn't change, you're back in jail. Let's go deeper than that. What else didn't change?"

"Our Belief Window."

I said, "If you want to get out of here and stay out, what do you have to do surgery on while you're here?"

"We've got to change our Belief Window."

A craggy-faced inmate came up to me at the end, tears streaming down his face. He shook my hand, looked me in the eye and said, "Hyrum, you've given me the key to how

I'm going to get out of here tonight." I wasn't sure how to take that. But he was excited.

Step 2. Identify Possible Principles Driving The Behavior:

I use the word "possible" because you are not going to become a psychologist when you finish this book. So how do we do step two? You start asking the question 'Why'. Will you write the word "why" next to number two, and then put a circle around the word "why." Why what? Why the behavior? Why are you wearing long hair, why are you smoking pot? Think about the answer.

The answer to the question, 'why,' always surfaces in the form of a principle on a Belief Window. Always.

Step 3. Predict Future Behavior Based on Those Principles

This is a wonderful model to study history with. Years before we got into the Second World War, did we know what Adolf Hitler had on his Belief Window? We knew. How did we know? He wrote a book. He told us. Could we have predicted his behavior knowing that? A lot of people did predict it. It was so ugly no one would believe it for about six years.

One of the principles on Hitler's Belief Window was that the races are graded. There are higher races and lower races. What was the highest race for Adolf Hitler? Aryans.

61

The lowest races were Jews and Blacks. Could we predict his behavior knowing he believed that?

Did the results of his behavior meet his needs over time? How long did the Thousand Year Reich last? Twelve years. Fifty million lives, because of one messed up Belief Window.

Do we know what Osama bin Laden had on his Belief Window? We know. How do we know? He wrote about it as a teenager. Do you know who he believed he was? He believed he was the re-incarnate of Saladin. Saladin, in the 12th century, broke the back of the Crusades. He was probably one of the best field commanders in military history. That is who bin Laden believed he was. Take that through the model. If that's true then, what is it bin Laden had to do? He had to kill the infidels. Where are the infidels? Wherever 'non-believers' are.

Do you know who Saddam Hussein believed he was? He believed he was the re-incarnate of Nebuchadnezzar. Look at history. Nebuchadnezzar was a Persian king that killed thousands of people and conquered the then known world. That's who Saddam thought he was.

Do we know what Benjamin Franklin, John Adams, Thomas Jefferson, and George Washington had on their Belief Windows? We know. How do we know? They wrote them down. We have their letters and writings, and ultimately the Constitution of the United States.

Steps Four through Six

Step 4: Identify alternative principles. This is where healing begins.

Step 5: Predict future behavior based on the new principles.

Step 6: Compare steps three and five.

Ask yourself which set of predicted behaviors makes the most sense?

Young people pick up on this with lightning speed. We adopted another school in Salt Lake called the Redwood Elementary School. It's an at risk school. Half the children show up without shoes and coats in the winter. Many of them only have one parent. It's a pretty tough area. So we adopted the school. Our colleagues at FranklinCovey spend a lot of time there.

Once I went there to speak to the 5th and 6th graders of the Redwood Elementary School. These kids were little, ten or eleven years old. There were 150 of them sitting on the floor of the cafeteria. I spoke to them for 90 minutes. I made them take notes. I came back to my office and thought, "Man, those kids hate me. They'll never have me back. Did they even understand what I was talking about?"

Three weeks later I was in a service station, midway between my office and their school. I was putting gas in my car. Out of nowhere, a little Polynesian kid came around the back of my car and said, "Hey, is that going to meet your needs over time?"

He got it. He got it.

If you have teenagers in your home, teach them the model. You will discover that you now have a way of talking to that teenager in a way that you're not attacking them. You're sitting, side-by-side, looking at their Belief Window.

Failure Is Part Of Growth

I have traveled a great deal over the past many years. Since I had spent so much time away from home, one day my wife approached me and said: "Hyrum, if I'm going to live alone anyway, why don't you let me live where I'd like to live?" Not a great way to start a conversation.

I had just less than six million miles on commercial aircraft. I asked, "Well, where would you like to live?"

My wife grew up in southern Utah. She really wanted to live where she grew up. So we moved to St. George, in the southern part of the state. My office was 312 miles from our house.

After we arrived in St. George, my son got onto the High School basketball team. He developed a peculiar behavior. Every time he'd shoot a ball in a game and miss, he'd stop shooting for the rest of the game. If he ran into one of the other players, he'd back off and stop being aggressive. If he received a bad grade in school, he would

64

implode. He would get real ugly when he got bad grades. This was his behavior.

My son understands the Reality Model. Why? I've burned it into his brain. He has it tattooed to his right thigh. (Joke) Now remember, I'm not going to attack my son, what am I going to attack? Something he can fix. His Belief Window.

So on a Sunday morning I sat down with my son. We were still in our pajamas.

I said, "Joseph, can I share with you some behavior that I've been observing?" (Step one) I didn't say step one, but he knew what was happening.

Then I said, "Could we then identify some possible principles that might be driving that behavior?" (Step two)

He responded, "Sure, Dad, what's the problem?" He wasn't threatened at all.

"Well, son, here's your behavior. Every time you shoot a ball in a game and miss, you stop shooting for the rest of the game. You've got the best shot on the team and you stop shooting. When you run into one of the other players you back off and stop being aggressive. When you get a bad grade in school you get real ugly."

I then moved to step two and started asking the question why. Why do you back off? Why do you stop shooting? Why do you get so ugly when you get bad grades?"

Now this didn't happen fast. Remember, the answer always comes up in the form of a principle on a Belief Window. There were all kinds of weird principles on that kid's Belief Window. But your gut tells you when you get to the big one, bedrock.

Twenty-five minutes into this conversation, my son sat there in a very reflective mood, he looked at me and said, "Well, Dad, I think you need to understand, I am really afraid of failing."

A big red flag went up in my brain.

I said, "Joseph, I think we've found the principle on your Belief Window and the principle is 'failure is bad'. Where did you get a principle like that?" My son looked up at me. He didn't have to say anything.

Where did he get it? From me his dad. He immediately became emotional. "Come on, Dad, you don't know anything about failure."

"What do you mean I don't know anything about failure?"

He was shaking. "You can't even spell failure, Dad. You go all over the world giving speeches! Everybody thinks you're terrific. You've got your own private plane for crying out loud! You don't know anything about failure."

I said, "Listen, kid, let me tell you about my failures."

I then spent 90 minutes detailing my personal failures. Five major financial disasters. I made the mistake of telling him about my grades in school. I recommend you don't do that, by the way, but I did.

When I finished, he looked at me and said, "You mean it's okay to fail, Dad?"

"Yeah, it's okay, son, all you have to do is fix it after you've messed up."

We put a new principle on his Belief Window that day about failure. And the new principle is 'failure is part of growth.' Two days later I watched him play in another basketball game. He started shooting when he shouldn't shoot. He was lobbing 40-foot shots. He started to enjoy hurting the other team.

The coach had to pull him out of the game. "You're going to hurt somebody, kid, you're an animal, now sit down."

He came home one day with a D on an exam, triumphant: "I got a D, Dad, have you ever seen one of those?" I had.

We had to have a whole new conversation about grades and Belief Windows. But, the minute he placed a new principle on his Belief Window about failure, a lot of pain went out of his life.

Teaching this model to those we know and love can drastically change the trajectory of their life. When a Belief Window is changed to 'failure is okay as long as you fix it,' then tremendous growth and learning can begin. Why? Because we learn to identify why we are getting the results we get – by principles on our Belief Windows.

Chapter 4
Belief Window Issues

From the previous chapter we saw examples of people throughout history who had different Belief Windows. The principles on those Belief Windows had some devastating results in some situations and some tremendously positive and fulfilling results in others. See if you can identify if the people in the previous chapter were pessimists, optimists, or realists.

Pessimist, Optimist, and Realist

Let's take a look at three more definitions: The pessimist, the optimist and the realist. These are Belief Window issues. Admiral James Stockdale, in Vietnam was the highest-ranking officer to spend six years as a prisoner in Hanoi. In his book 'Good to Great,', Jim Collins talks about the Stockdale paradox. Stockdale discovered three distinct groups in the prison in Hanoi: pessimists, optimists, and realists. He discovered the same three groups of people that Viktor Frankl discovered at Auschwitz during the Second World War. These are Stockdale's definitions:

The pessimist sees the brutal facts and quits.

The optimist has boundless faith and ignores the brutal facts.

The realist sees the brutal facts and has faith they can be dealt with.

Realists Survive

The first two groups never came home from Hanoi. The first two groups never got out of Auschwitz. They died there.

I understand why the pessimists died. They saw the brutal facts: "We're in the middle of southeast Asia, we are 8,000 miles from home, there is no way the Marines are going to get in here and save us, we're toast, guys" and they gave up and died. A lot of physically able people died.

The optimists surprised me. Why would the optimists die? They have boundless faith. They say, "Hey guys, we're going to be out of here by Christmas. If we're not out of here by Christmas we'll be out of here by Valentine's." They ignored the brutal facts. "We're in the middle of Southeast Asia, we're 8,000 miles from home. There's no way anybody's going to get in here." When they weren't out by Christmas and they weren't out by Valentine's, what happened to the second group? They became pessimists and died.

The realists survived. Why? They saw the brutal facts: "We're in the middle of Southeast Asia, we're 8,000 miles from home, the Marines are not coming in here. Guys, we're going to be here for a long time, so let's get together and make it." They had faith they could deal with it. Some pretty emaciated bodies survived because of that.

So the issue is, what are you? This is a Belief Window issue. Are we experiencing any kind of adversity right now in our country? Are there any brutal facts we have to deal with in our country right now and globally? How about your own family?

A Principle To Ponder:

I'm going to ask you now to consider a principle for your Belief Window. I discovered this principle many years ago when I lost a daughter and a granddaughter in a car accident. It was a very difficult time for my wife and me. Let me introduce the principle with this experience.

About three or four weeks after 9-11, I received a call from the office of Rudi Giuliani, then the mayor of New York City. He said, "Hyrum, we've got a lot of people in pain here because of what happened on 9-11. Would you and your partner Stephen Covey come and do a full day workshop for the families affected by 9-11."

I said, "Of course we'll do it."

They said, "The Midtown Sheraton Hotel's going to donate the ballroom and they'll donate your room, but we can't pay you."

"Fine."

We flew to New York on the 18th of October, six weeks after 9-11. I've flown into New York hundreds of times. This was different. The World Trade Center was gone.

The next morning, the mayor arranged for a tour of Ground Zero. It was just Franklin Covey CEO Bob

Whitman, Stephen Covey and me. A policeman picked us up at five o'clock and we drove down to Ground Zero. You could not get anywhere near Ground Zero at that point because 1600 policemen cordoned it off. We went through four checkpoints to get to Ground Zero.

About a quarter past five we were standing at Ground Zero on 15 feet of compacted debris. We were looking at this huge hole. You can't imagine the size of that hole unless you were there. I've taught lots of seminars in the World Trade Center. I couldn't believe it could be gone.

The policeman who was our escort started to tell us his story. He was very animated.

"I was here that day." He pointed, "I was standing right over there. All of a sudden I heard this big boom and I looked up and all this stuff came flying out of the World Trade Center. It looked like paper at first, and then it started hitting the ground. It was 50 foot I-beams, killing everybody they hit. I watched 34 people jump from the tower. Four of them were holding hands when they jumped. I watched eight firemen lose their lives because people fell on them."

He looked at me and asked, "Mr. Smith, how many computers do you think there were in the World Trade Center?"

I said, "Well, a lot. 50,000 people worked in the World Trade Center."

"We haven't found one computer."

"Really, how come?"

"A three thousand degree fire, and it is still burning."

72

While he was talking, a crane pulled an I-beam out of the rubble, it was dripping molten steel at the bottom, six weeks after the explosion.

The policeman continued, "You know, when that second building came down, we all thought we were dead, but I crawled under a truck and somehow I survived."

That's how our morning started. We went back up to the Midtown Sheraton. We had to shower because we were covered with soot. We came down to the ballroom which was designed for 1,800 people. There were 2,400 people jammed into it. The meeting began with two policemen and two firemen dressed in dress uniforms marching in with the American flag. That wiped me out. Then the Harlem Girls Choir marched in and sang three patriotic songs. Sixty beautiful young women. They blew the roof off the place. I was a mess. I was grateful Stephen Covey spoke first.

So Dr. Covey got up and did his thing. Then it was my turn. I made my way to the front of the ballroom. People were sitting on the floor. Before I could open my mouth, about halfway back in the ballroom a fireman jumped out of his chair, shouted at me and said, "Mr. Smith, are you going tell us how to get out of bed in the morning when we just don't give a crap anymore?"

That's how it started. This turned out to be one of the toughest, and yet most rewarding, speaking experiences I have ever had.

I said these words to the fireman, and this is what I want you to ponder:

Pain is inevitable; misery is optional.

What principle—what point am I trying to make here? The fact is, bad things happen to good people, do they not? The fact is we're not going to get through this mortal experience without some pain. How we choose to deal with that pain is ultimately dependent on what stays on our Belief Window. And by the way, the thing that separates you and me from the rest of the animal kingdom is that we can change our beliefs. We're in charge of our Belief Window."

And then I taught this group exactly what I've taught you in this book. It was an electrifying experience.

When I finished, I said, "I will never minimize or put down what happened here on 9-11. This was bad. But just for a moment, would you compare what happened here on 9-11 to what's happened on this planet in the last one hundred and fifty years. What happened here on 9-11 doesn't even come up on the scope of ugliness, compared to other events in that period. Does it?"

"Let's go back to June 6th, 1944. No, let's go back to June 5th, 1944. Eisenhower was in a bunker in England. You know what he said to his generals? He wrote about this in his memoirs. He said, 'Gentlemen, we've got to throw more kids at that beach tomorrow than they have bullets in the bunker.' He estimated within 500 how many he'd lose. So you know what they did the next day? They threw 200,000 kids at that beach in France. Do you know what happened? The Nazis ran out of bullets in the bunker. How often do we reverence that?

Iwo Jima was supposed to be a four-day battle in the Pacific. It lasted 36 days. There were 8,000 Marines dead and 20,000 wounded. There were 22,000 Japanese soldiers killed. How often do we reverence that? The killing fields in Cambodia were in the millions. Stalin killed 50 million of his own people.

Pain is inevitable, misery is optional.

Some of the most serene, magnificent, amazing and wonderful people I have ever known are people who have gone through excruciating pain. But they decided not to be miserable. And by deciding not to be miserable, they don't make other people miserable with them. You know what the neat thing about 9-11 was? You couldn't buy a flag in America for about 9 months and it was also okay for a man to cry.

Are you an optimist, a pessimist, or a realist? We may be all three at various times depending on the situation. If we begin applying this model we should start to recognize which of the three we are, in each situation. Gaining this skill will add tremendous value to our personal lives, as well as those we come in contact with. In conclusion I want to share with you a few lines from an inspiring piece of literature.

Chapter 5
Inner Peace

As I mentioned earlier, we are all after inner peace. You have learned the Reality Model, heard examples, and learned the steps to apply it. In this final chapter you will see an example that sums up much of what may go on inside someone's head when they think about the results of future behavior.

The Rape of Lucrece

Would you please think about this Shakespeare poem? The poem illustrates what we're talking about. What if every time you had to make a decision, for good or for ill, these words came to into your mind?

"What win I, if I gain the thing I seek?" How would it change the way you see the results?

This poem is about a man by the name of Lucius Tarquinius Superbus (535 – 496 BC) who was the legendary seventh and final King of Rome. He was thinking about raping the beautiful Lucrece. While he was thinking about this ugly, foul deed, these words come into his mind:

What win I if I gain the thing I seek?
A dream, a breath, a froth of fleeting joy?
Who buys a minute's mirth to wail a week?

Or sells eternity to get a toy?
For one sweet grape who would the vine destroy?
Or what fond beggar but to touch the crown
would with the scepter, straight, be stricken down?"

Meeting Your Needs Over Time

You may never remember this poem in its entirety but always remember the first line. **"What win I if I gain the thing I seek?" Will the results of your behavior meet your needs over time?** Shakespeare understood this idea many hundreds of years ago. This is a very old idea. If every person understood the power of their perceptions and how those perceptions affect reality, what kind of decisions will they make? What decisions will you make now that you understand that power?

If you can learn nothing more from this book than to start asking yourself this question or by quoting the first line of "The Rape of Lucrece" to help ground you, it will bring you a step closer to see a marked and measurable change in how you make personal and professional decisions. And what if you taught your children this concept of beliefs and perceptions? You'll be changing the course of history.

I should tell you that six weeks after we went through that experience with the tough students at the high school, I got a call from the drug and alcohol specialist of that school district.

The first thing out of his mouth was, "What did you do to those kids?"

"What do you mean? I almost didn't survive that."

He said, "Listen, ten of those kids have completely turned around."

JD was one of them. Eventually JD graduated from high school. Nobody thought he would. He went to college, he's now married, has a couple of children and he understands and is teaching his own kids to understand the Power of Perception.

Afterword

At the beginning of the book I asked you to commit to doing three things:

1. Take notes.

2. Ponder your notes for 36 hours after reading the book.

3. Within 48 hours of finishing the book, teach it to someone else.

I promise that if you will do these three things you will see a marked and measurable change in how you make personal and professional decisions. I've told you many stories of how understanding and applying the model has caused powerful change in people's lives. The decision is now yours to use the model and see what impact you can have on those around you.

I'd love to hear from you. Send me your stories and your experiences with the Reality Model.

You can connect with me on:

- My website: www.hyrumwsmith.com
- Facebook: www.facebook.com/hyrumwsmith
- Twitter: www.twitter.com/hyrumwsmith

Join my community so I can continue to connect with you.

Hyrum W. Smith

About the Author

Hyrum W. Smith is a distinguished author, speaker, and businessman. Hyrum W. Smith is the Co-Founder and former CEO of Franklin Covey, Co. For three decades he has been empowering people to effectively govern their personal and professional lives. Hyrum's books and presentations have been acclaimed by American and international audiences. He combines wit and enthusiasm with a gift for communicating compelling principles that incite lasting personal change.

Hyrum is the author of several nationally-acclaimed books, including *The 10 Natural Laws of Successful Time and Life Management, What Matters Most, The Advanced Day Planner User's Guide, and The Modern Gladiator. He also co-authored Excellence Through Time Management.*

After serving in the United States Army as the field commander of a Pershing missile battery in Germany, Hyrum graduated from Brigham Young University in 1971.

In 1984 he became one of the original creators of the popular Franklin Day Planner. He also co-founded the Franklin Quest Company to produce the planner and train individuals and organizations in the time management principles on which the planner was based.

Hyrum served as Vice-Chairman of the Board of Franklin Covey Company, Franklin Quest's successor, until 2004.

Hyrum has received numerous honors and community service awards, including the following:

- International Entrepreneur of the Year by Brigham Young University's Marriott School of Management in 1993
- Three honorary doctorate degrees
- SRI Gallup Hall of Fame and Man of the Year Award in 1992
- Silver Beaver Award from the Boy Scouts of America

He also serves on several boards of directors and national advisory councils.

After growing up in Honolulu, Hawaii, Hyrum met his wife, Gail, met in London, England in 1965. He returned from London and was drafted into the army.

They were married in 1966 while Hyrum was on leave. They have 6 children (5 living) and 20 grandchildren (18 living).

Hyrum enjoys golfing, shooting pistols and rifles, listening to classical music, horse riding and spending time with his family at his ranch in southern Utah.